The
Book of Life

The
Book of Life

The Master Key to Inner Peace and Relationship Harmony

A New Interpretation of Epictetus's *Handbook*

EDITED AND INTERPRETED FOR A NEW MILLENNIUM
BY GAY HENDRICKS AND PHILIP JOHNCOCK

HAY HOUSE, INC.
Carlsbad, California
London • Sydney • Johannesburg
Vancouver • Hong Kong • New Delhi

Published and distributed in the United States by: Hay House, Inc.: www.hayhouse.com • **Published and distributed in Australia by:** Hay House Australia Pty. Ltd.: www.hayhouse.com.au • **Published and distributed in the United Kingdom by:** Hay House UK, Ltd.: www.hayhouse.co.uk • **Published and distributed in the Republic of South Africa by:** Hay House SA (Pty), Ltd.: orders@psdprom.co.za • **Distributed in Canada by:** Raincoast: www.raincoast.com • **Published in India by:** Hay House Publications (India) Pvt. Ltd.: www.hayhouseindia.co.in • **Distributed in India by:** Media Star: booksdivision@mediastar.co.in

Editorial supervision: Jill Kramer • *Design:* Tricia Breidenthal

Library of Congress Control No.: 2005921158

ISBN 13: 978-1-4019-0770-9
ISBN 10: 1-4019-0770-9

09 08 07 06   4 3 2 1
1st printing, July 2006

Printed in the United States of America

To the memory of my grandfather, E. R. Canaday, who lived and breathed the wisdom of Epictetus.

— Gay Hendricks

CONTENTS

INTRODUCTION

Epictetus's remarkable *Handbook* has been passed lovingly from one spiritual seeker to another for 2,000 years. Now, with great pleasure, we place it in your hands. As you savor its nourishing wisdom—radiantly clear from its first sentence to its last—you'll understand why emperors have carried it with them in war and peace, and ordinary citizens from every walk of life have treasured it as well. In modern times, an American prisoner of war who spent five years in a cell in Hanoi kept himself sane by recalling and applying the wisdom of this book. In assessing its impact on the Western heart and mind, many people consider it second only to the Bible in its influence.

Every person we've ever known who has been touched by this book feels fortunate, even graced, to have heard its message. When you know a bit about its history, you'll understand just how lucky we are that it survived the centuries. For starters, Epictetus didn't write down a word of the *Handbook* himself. According to history, this remarkable collection of wisdom was gathered by his students from his oral teachings. One student, Arrian, put it all together into the volume you now hold, and it was originally called *Enchiridion* (which in Greek means "close to hand," but is usually translated as "manual" or "handbook").

It's even something of a miracle that Epictetus got to speak these words. He was born in Phrygia (now part of Turkey) as a slave, which is never an easy challenge to overcome. The story goes that he actually limped to Rome in a slave caravan because his knee had been shattered by beatings and was left untreated. Fortunately, his genius eventually came to light, and even though he wasn't a free man, he was allowed to study philosophy with one of the city's great teachers. Epictetus went on to found his own school of conscious living, which attracted many well-connected students. He became known as one of the greatest stoic philosophers, and his ideas influenced some of the loftiest Roman thinkers, including the emperor Marcus Aurelius.

Epictetus lived during a time of incredible turbulence in the Roman Empire, which was being rocked from within by political revolts and threatened from outside by barbarians. When the emperor Domitian, a strict fundamentalist in the religion of ancient Rome, banished the philosophers, Epictetus was forced to relocate to Greece, accompanied by a band of passionate students. It was here that the material in this book was lovingly collected.

Now, nearly two millennia later, the concepts in the book still serve us as brilliantly as they did so long ago. While we've edited the *Handbook* for clarity—updating the language and omitting more obscure references— we've done our best to remain true to the message of the original text. As you read Parts I and II of this book, you'll surely see how deeply Epictetus's ideas have penetrated the transformational literature of our time. For example, the Serenity Prayer, repeated millions of times a day by members of 12-step programs, is based almost verbatim on his teachings. The modern therapy techniques of cognitive behavior modification are also heavily influenced by his words.

But what gives this small book such a big power to change lives? The answer is in the very first sentence: "You can be happy if you know this master-secret: Some things are within your power to control and some things aren't." To understand the meaning and implications of these first few words is to make a transformational shift that can be used in every life situation, no matter how troublesome or trivial.

Many people consider this basic concept the master-secret of transformation, because it can be applied in a life-changing way to any situation. For example, you might be grieving over the loss of a loved one. Months have gone by and you still can't shake the sadness. You've talked to friends, counselors, and family, yet the sadness remains. One day you pick up this little book, and by inner guidance or just good luck, you read the first sentence. You take a few deep breaths and let its wisdom suffuse you, and then begin to comprehend that the fact of the loss is far outside your power to change. You can't control it! As this sinks in, you see that you've been expending massive energy trying to alter the past. You've been attempting to rewrite reality, and the exertion is exhausting you. You let go of the futile effort and feel a new peace spreading through you.

Suddenly, an even deeper understanding sinks in: You realize that you've been engaged in a battle to control the emotions of grief and sadness in your own body. You've been trying to minimize them, eliminate them, and get over them. Even your family and friends, with the very best of intentions, have been trying to talk you out of your feelings. You've been attempting to manage things that are fundamentally uncontrollable, and the cost has been the moment-by-moment disruption of your peace of mind. Your inner experience since the loss has been somewhat like driving a car with one foot on the accelerator and the other on the brake: You've felt nothing but an unsettling inner shimmy, and the rattle has unnerved your every moment.

But now, with the help of Epictetus's manual, you see the futility of trying to control your emotions. They have a life of their own, and they'll last as long as they last. Applying the wisdom Epictetus conveys in his first sentence, you relax your resistance and let go of your effort to wish your feelings away. A whole-body, whole-being serenity begins to spread through you, and it feels very, very good.

This sequence of events actually happened to one of us (Gay Hendricks), with exactly the same result. Gay recalls, "Once, in a time of deep sadness over the loss of a child I'd loved and held in my arms nearly every day for the six months she was with us, I felt despair about ever being able to get out from under the cloud of grief that engulfed me. Yet part of me knew that I needed to dispel the fog of anguish so I could be present for others who needed me. It was then that I picked up an ancient, battered edition of Epictetus. I read the first few lines, and everything became clear. Suddenly I saw that I'd been trying with every fiber of my being to change something that I had no power over. I'd been straining to undo death. It seemed as if I'd been at a stalemate with the universe itself, and I can't describe the feeling of calm that rushed over me when I finally let go. I still felt the sadness, of course, but now I was at peace with it—I could simply let it be. For me it was the essential first step in moving beyond the devastating experience."

You can learn to apply the elegant simplicity of this master-secret in any situation. In fact, it's the subject of an experiential process in the last section of this book (you'll also find an audio version on the CD included in this edition). We call it the Master-Key Experiential Activity because it fits so many life situations. Even if you're not usually drawn to doing experiential processes, we highly recommend that you take the 30 or so minutes necessary to work through it. We predict that you'll come to think of it as one of the best investments of your time you've ever made.

The rich wisdom in this book is very distilled. In fact, it's *essential*—it contains the very core of what human beings really need to know. For this reason we recommend that its nourishing concepts be sipped and savored and enjoyed at leisure, not hurried or rushed through. Give it your loving attention, and it will reward you with the keys to a loving life.

— Gay Hendricks and Philip Johncock

PART I

THE TEXT OF
EPICTETUS'S
HANDBOOK

1

Y̲ou can be happy if you know this master-secret: Some things are within your power to control and some aren't. Your opinions are your own, you can choose the actions you take, and you're always in charge of where you place your attention. But you don't have any say over what goes on in someone else's body, so there's no way you can manage another person's feelings or thoughts.

When you focus on the things you *can* control, you give yourself the gift of independence—you'll be unhindered and part of the natural flow of the universe. By contrast, when you waste your energy on things you can't change, it inevitably weakens your sense of connection to the universal current and results in a sense of being enslaved and at the mercy of others. You play the role of the victim and you think, *Somebody did this to me.*

2

When you imagine that something is within your control when it isn't, you hamper and disturb the natural flow of energy in and around you. You begin to blame others—even God—for what's happening to you. However, if you turn your attention toward the things that you can change, and withdraw your efforts from what you can't, then no one has any power over you. Nobody *can* hinder your progress toward getting what you want. You stop blaming those around you for your situation and you cease to do things you don't want to. Your enemies even fade away, believe it or not. Ultimately, no one can harm you because you don't let their actions affect you.

3

To achieve everything you want, it isn't enough to be just moderately motivated or partially committed. A halfhearted effort never works. For example, you can't just let go of your fears about other people's opinions of you some of the time, and you can't postpone taking charge of your life until a later date. If you want to be happy and free, you need to dive right in and take responsibility for the things under your control and let go of the things that aren't. Then, if you get off track, you need to recommit.

4

Wisdom is the result of knowing the difference between what's going on in your head and reality. When something negative comes to mind, first realize that it's only a thought. Then ask yourself, *Is this something I have power over?* If what came up is beyond your control, be ready to reply, *This is something I can't change.*

It all begins with your ability to differentiate between your thinking and what's really going on in the world around you. To know that a thought is just a thought is at first unsettling, then massively liberating.

5

Remember that when you desire something, you're working toward attaining whatever it is you want. Likewise, you try to stay away from those things you have an aversion to. If you don't get what you hope for, it's unfortunate, but if you get what you're trying to steer clear of, you experience misfortune. That's why you should confine your avoidance to things within your control, so you'll never experience misery. Because if you try to sidestep sickness, death, or poverty, then sooner or later you're sure to run into them.

If you wish that your children, spouse, or friends would live forever, you want something that isn't up to you. Similarly, if you expect one of your employees to do perfect work, you're asking for that which is out of your hands. Don't try to elude circumstances that you have no power over; instead, exert your energy in areas where you have authority. Life becomes very easy then.

6

When you're fond of someone or something, be clear about what it is that you like. For example, if you have a certain vase that you treasure, say, "This is just a ceramic vase." That way, if it ever breaks, you'll keep your loss in perspective.

7

Before you take any action, be conscious of what it is that you're about to do. So if you're going to a public swimming pool, think about what commonly happens at these places. Children splash and play and yell, and some people may even steal unattended belongings. All of these things are part of going to the pool—you could even say they're part of the price of admission.

Conscious living invites you to say, "I want to go for a swim and also keep my choice in harmony with nature." Then, if anything unpleasant happens while you're there, remind yourself, "I didn't just want to go for a dip; I also wanted to keep my agreement to be at peace with the world around me. Acting from anger in response to what happens means that I'm not keeping my pact with myself and the universe."

8

It's not the events of your life that upset you; it's your judgment about what's happened. For example, dying scares a lot of people. The terror lies in our beliefs about the concept of death, that it's something horrible.

Whenever you're frustrated, disturbed, or upset, don't hold others responsible. If you're going to lay blame on anything, lay it on your own judgments. You see, an ignorant person holds others accountable for their lack of education, and someone who has begun the learning process believes they're responsible. But the fully educated person doesn't accuse others or oneself.

9

Have you ever boasted about a quality that wasn't yours? If a horse bragged about its beauty, perhaps by saying "I'm so lovely," then that would make sense. But when you gloat, "I have a beautiful horse," know that you're only praising the excellence of the horse, not yourself. Instead, say, "The horse is beautiful." This is more accurate.

What qualities best describe you right now? Friendly, gentle, strong, or solid? When you appreciate your own characteristics, you'll notice an increase in your vitality, and you'll also be in closer harmony with the laws of nature.

10

Let's consider this analogy: You're on a trip and your boat is anchored in a harbor. You go ashore to get water, and on the way, you stop to pick up some fresh fruit at a market. As you shop, remember to keep your thoughts fixed on the ship. Look back continually in case the captain should call. Then, if he does, toss aside your groceries. Otherwise you risk missing the boat.

Such is life. Instead of some fruit, you may pick up a spouse or a child. Neither of these should hinder you. If the captain (a metaphor for God) calls, leave everything and run to the ship without even looking back. And if you're old, don't wander far from the ship—when it's time to go aboard, it may take you longer to get there.

11

Instead of asking for things to happen as you wish, wish for them to happen as they are. Your life will go smoothly because you'll be in harmony with what is.

12

Sickness may slow down your body, but it doesn't need to interfere with your conscious choices. If you injure your leg, it's only one part of you that's hurt. If you allow your wound to affect your ability to choose, then where's your power? You've given it away. But when you take responsibility for what happens in your life, the opposite happens—all hindrances disappear.

13

When you consider your life's circumstances, ask, "What can I learn from this?" and "How can I use this knowledge?" Here are several examples: Beauty teaches self-control, pain teaches endurance, and abuse teaches patience. When you stay open to how you created your present condition and gain new understanding, you center and ground yourself, creating space and wonder so that what you most want and need magically appears. When you ask yourself the two questions above, you quicken the time it takes for you to absorb the valuable lessons you set up—and then move on.

14

Have you ever found yourself worrying over something that you lost—perhaps a relationship that broke up or a job you got laid off from? You could perceive it as a loss, but you could also think about it in another way—as something you've given back.

Instead of saying, "I've lost it," say, "I've returned it." It was never yours in the first place. You were a steward of it, temporarily. For example, if the money you had in the stock market disappears, it was given back. The same is true even if your marriage dissolves or your child dies.

"But what if the person who stole this thing from me is evil?" you ask. The fact of the matter is, it doesn't matter how the giver demands something back. As long as it's in your possession, take care of it. Treat it as something not your own, the way that travelers treat an inn.

15

If you want to be happy, let go of your conditional thinking, such as, *If I quit my job, then I won't be able to pay my bills,* or *If I don't punish my son, then he won't learn the difference between right and wrong.* Conditional thinking usually follows the formula: *If I _____, then _____ will happen.*

Start with the little things. Did your car get scratched in a parking lot? Did someone steal your wallet? Say to yourself, *This is the price paid for peace of mind, for freedom from disturbance, and nothing is without cost.* It's far better to die of hunger but free of grief and fear than to live with great wealth and anxiety.

16

If you want to be truly happy, cultivate indifference about what others think of you. It doesn't matter if they believe you're foolish, stupid, or even intelligent. The point is, beware of how you view yourself.

17

Imagine that you're at a dinner party with a group of friends and a tray of appetizers is being passed around. Don't move across the room to get one. Wait, and when it comes your way, reach out your hand and take a moderate portion.

My advice to you is that you don't stretch out your desire toward an object, but rather wait for it to come to you. This is the secret to attracting abundance. When you allow something—a job, wealth, or even a spouse or a child—to flow toward you, rather than grab from a needy place, you're worthy to share your life with the gods.

18

Have you ever been around someone weeping and grieving over the loss of a relationship, a job, property, or even a loved one? Realize that it isn't what has happened that's upsetting this person, but his or her judgment about it. At the same time, it's important to show compassion and resonate with what's going on. You might say something such as, "I imagine that you're feeling deep sadness." But don't take on the pain as your own when it's not yours.

19

You've probably heard it said that life is a stage and we're merely the actors. You see, any play is as short or as long as the playwright wants to make it, and he or she chooses the roles—whether you're rich or poor, a celebrity or an average citizen, or have a handicap or not. Your job is to fully play out your part, and also realize that the playwright chose it for you.

20

Some people are superstitious. They avoid black cats crossing the road, never walk under ladders, and see ravens cawing as inauspicious omens—prophetic signs of bad things to come. It's important to draw a distinction and say something like, "None of these signs affect me, my family, my reputation, or anything else associated with me." Instead, imagine that all omens are positive—that is, if you choose them to be. Affirm, "All omens are lucky because I see them as such. For whatever happens, it will be for my highest good."

21

When you see someone honored above you, in a position of great power, or reveling in their achievement, don't get carried away by the images of success you project or your judgment that he or she is better off than you are. The essence of good lies in what you can control, so there's no room for either envy or jealousy.

Again, the only way to true freedom and happiness is to avoid, perhaps even despise, whatever you can't change. Don't try to be anything you're not; instead, just try to be free. The only way to do this is to let go of the things you have no power over.

22

Have you even been in a situation where someone has insulted or provoked you? Most people have. Bear in mind that what's truly irritating in such a circumstance isn't the person who's offending you, it's your judgment about how you're being treated.

So when someone aggravates you, realize that it's your own feelings that are bothering you, not the other person. Avoid giving your attention and energy to your emotions—you might even take a few deep breaths. If you can do this, you'll create time and space for yourself to get centered again.

23

Here's a trick for transforming your deepest fear into joy: Every day, imagine your greatest terror—whether it's death, torture, exile, or whatever. Facing your anxiety brings clarity to your thoughts and innermost desires, and it also creates space for your life purpose to appear, effortlessly and magically.

24

If you express your genius in the world and ask for what you truly desire, be prepared to be ridiculed. Some people may say, "Who do you think you are?" or "You're so selfish." Hold fast to the essence of who you are and what you most want, as if you've been appointed by God to this position. If you're true to your path, the very same people who laughed at you will come to admire you. But if you give in to their abuse, you'll be mocked twice over.

25

When you live to please others, you waste valuable time and energy on that which is beyond your control. When you notice your attention going toward placating others (which is impossible anyway), stop. Then recommit to putting yourself first and taking responsibility for the things that you *can* change.

2 6

As you now know so well, some events in life are beyond your control. They just occur, and there's no sense in beating yourself up over them. If your neighbor's child broke a glass, you'd likely say, "Don't worry—things happen." Why don't you have this same attitude when *you* accidentally break something?

You can apply this same principle to greater things, too. Has a relationship ended? Have you been laid off from your job? Has a loved one died? Rather than losing yourself in grief, make a shift by telling yourself what you'd say to a friend if he or she were in the same situation. That way you become a good neighbor to yourself.

Is it within your power to determine whether you get promoted at work? No. You can certainly influence your boss's decision, but ultimately it's out of your hands. Can you control whether you get invited to a party? Absolutely not—the host or hostess makes up the guest list.

Instead of struggling with what you don't have a say in, focus on living with integrity. If you do, the whole world around you will benefit.

27

How you behave is often determined by your social roles and relationships. For example, you're taught that because a man is your father, you should listen to his instructions, value his authority, and care for him when he's aging. But what if he's a neglectful father? Are you entitled to a caring one? No, you're only given a father, period.

The same holds true for a sister or any other relation. If you maintain the high road regardless of the other person's behavior, you keep your capacity for choice consistent with nature. You see, no one can hurt you unless you allow them to. You injure yourself when you think that you've been treated unkindly.

Decide how you'll treat others—neighbors, family members, and authority figures—and do just that, regardless of their behavior toward you.

28

Here's the secret to living in harmony: Let go of thinking of things as "good" and "evil." If you believe that any of the things that aren't up to you are either of these imposters, you'll undoubtedly blame and even despise others when you don't get what you want.

From now on, be aware of your tendency to judge people. Do you think your brother is inferior to you because he's not as tidy as you are? Do you say your mother's a bad person because she drinks? Unless you can get inside another person's mind and really see from their perspective, you can't know their intentions. You'll lose your ability to appreciate others if you let your judgments get in the way.

29

Socrates thought that you should resort to divination in cases where your survival rides on the outcome or you've exhausted all other options—such as when someone seeks a shaman to help them heal from a terminal disease. Whenever you decide to have your future told by a psychic, astrologer, or other diviner, remember that you don't know what's going to happen in your life until this person tells you. But you can be sure that if it's an event out of your control, then by definition, it can't be good or evil.

So if you see a psychic, don't bring desire or aversion with you. Don't be afraid. Just clear your mind so that you'll be indifferent to any outcome. In other words, let go of judgment. But do know that whatever happens, it's always within your power to make choices—no one can hinder this. And if you've ever had a premonition or insight about a friend, go ahead and share what you know. You don't need to ask a psychic. Stand by your friend.

30

Now is a good time to establish a code of conduct for yourself, to determine how you'll act when you're alone and also when you're in the presence of others. Here's my advice based on my experience in the world: For the most part, be silent. Speak only when it's necessary. Avoid conversing about meaningless topics, such as sports, the weather, and parties. Above all else, don't gossip about people—whether you're praising, blaming, or comparing them to others. When you do talk, discuss things that are important and of interest to you.

Don't laugh too much. Try not to take oaths of any kind. Steer clear of vulgar people and entertainment, but if you can't, keep focused so that you don't slip into the same unrefined behavior.

When shopping for food, clothing, drink, housing, and other necessities of life, it's wise to be economical.

Take and use only as much as you really need, and resist the urge to show off.

If a friend tells you that someone is speaking badly of you, don't stoop to defend yourself. In fact, respond by saying, "That's interesting. But he must not know my other faults because he only mentioned these."

31

If you're tempted by some pleasure, don't let yourself be carried away without considering the possible consequences. You can imagine the fun you might have, but also call to mind the regret you'll experience if you're reckless. Don't put yourself in situations that aren't in your best interest.

When you do abstain from some indulgence, don't feel sorry for yourself. Instead, celebrate your wise decision.

32

When you do something that you wholeheartedly believe should be done, such as organizing a protest against drunk driving, know that some people may not like it. But why should you care about what others think when you're doing the right thing?

33

There are two sides to every coin. If your brother wrongs you, this is only one side. Remember that he is still your sibling, someone brought up in the same family as you. If you see both sides, you'll be able to bear him.

34

It doesn't make sense to say, "I'm richer than you; therefore, I'm superior to you," or "I'm more eloquent than you, which means I'm better than you." Being wealthy and well spoken doesn't have anything to do with how you're defined. You aren't greater than anyone; you just *are*.

35

It's best to live by example rather than to call yourself an expert and go around telling everyone else how to behave. For example, at a banquet, don't correct people's manners, but rather eat in the way that you believe everyone should.

Sheep don't throw up the grass to show the shepherds how much they've eaten. Instead, they digest their food internally, then produce wool and milk externally. Likewise, don't preach philosophy to laymen. Make sure that you get down to living your principles rather than merely talking about them.

36

When you adopt a simple life, don't brag about it. If you make a choice to discipline yourself, even to fast, do it for your own sake and not for anyone else. When you're struggling, think of the poor people in this world who are so much more patient in the face of hardship than the rest of us are. Then, when you're really thirsty, take a little cold water in your mouth and spit it out. There's no need to tell anyone that you did so.

37

Whatever commitments you make to yourself, abide by them as you would a law. Honor them as sacred. Don't worry about what others might think, because what they say is of no concern to you.

38

What are you waiting for? You're not a child any longer, but an adult who is going to take full responsibility for your life. Take this moment to make a commitment to follow reason and conscious-living precepts. You've decided to change how you see and relate to the world, and you owe yourself nothing less.

From this moment on, imagine that you're worthy of living happily and abundantly, in harmony with yourself and others. Let the best of everything come to you effortlessly. Welcome it!

You're competing in the true Olympics—real life. When anything burdensome, sweet, glorious, or otherwise comes up, acknowledge it, then recommit to living authentically. Your success comes from your willingness to make a single move or action that puts you back on the path of integrity.

PART II

THE LOST
FRAGMENTS OF
EPICTETUS

DISCOVERING THE LOST FRAGMENTS

Nowadays it's easy to stroll into a bookstore and walk out with an armload of very useful and sophisticated knowledge about how to change your life. But in the ancient world, such knowledge was hard to come by and more prized than diamonds. Depending on the whim of the current emperor, it could even be dangerous to pass on philosophical wisdom. Spiritual seekers were forced to hold secret meetings and pass Epictetus's teachings from hand to hand, to be studied late at night by candlelight. As a result, there are many fragments that are almost certain to be his words, although there's no way verify them as authentic. Here are a few of the most significant of these passages.

Fragment 1

How important is it to know that the universe is made up of atoms or molecules of water, fire, and earth? Even more important than this is to know the true nature of good and evil, the extent of your desires and aversions, and your impulses to act and not to act. What are the universal laws that order the affairs of your life, such as saying good-bye to those things that are beyond your control and concentrating on what's within your control?

Acknowledging your true personality and recognizing these universal laws is necessary in order to live a happy and prosperous life. The Delphic admonition—"Know thyself"—is key. Understanding Mother Nature, and how she governs the universe and whether she exists or not, isn't as important as an awareness of self.

If you told the singer in a chorus to know himself, wouldn't he use his environment and relationships—the

partners in the chorus and the music he sings—to do so?
Wouldn't the same be true for a soldier, a sailor, or anyone else?

Man lives all by himself and in relationship.

FRAGMENT 2

L oving what you have is the key first step to having what you want, just as learning to appreciate what's been given to you is important to the art of conscious living. The person who does this and acts rationally resonates with, and lives in, alignment with the laws of the universe.

FRAGMENT 3

It's universal law that all things obey and serve the universe—earth and sea, sun and stars, plants and animals. Your body, likewise, obey its laws, both in sickness and health, and youth and old age, as you pass through the stages of your life.

It's reasonable, then, that those things that obey and serve you, namely your judgments, obey and serve you *and* the universe. For the universe is powerful and superior to you, and it has done even more on your behalf than you can imagine by embracing you in its bigger picture of existence. To act against the universe is to align yourself with a lack of reason, futile harassment, pain, and sorrow.

FRAGMENT 4

Of everything that exists in the universe, God has given you some things that are within your power and some that aren't. The things you have control over are the finest and most excellent of things, which will bring you happiness and the ability to use your imagination. When you focus on these, you experience peace, freedom, cheerfulness, consistency, justice, law, self-control, and virtue.

You can entrust the things you can't change to the universe. If those things need your children, country, body, or anything else, I recommend that you gladly yield them to the greater power.

FRAGMENT 5

You've probably heard the biblical advice to "turn the other cheek." Well, do you know the story of Lycurgus the Spartan? He was blinded in one eye by one of his fellow countrymen. The people handed over the perpetrator to Lycurgus to take whatever vengeance he sought fit.

To many people's surprise, Lycurgus refrained from taking revenge, but instead educated the man and made a responsible person of him—even brought him to the theater. When asked why he did this, the Spartan replied, "This man was insolent and violent when I met him. I'm restoring him to you as a decent and good citizen."

FRAGMENT 6

The function of nature is above all else to restrain your impulses and bring them into harmony with what you judge to be useful and fitting.

Mean-spirited and foolish people believe that they're despised by others because they've had this as their primary experience thus far in their lives. Beware of those who don't have the capacity to do harm because they likely lack the capacity to help as well.

FRAGMENT 7

The key to living a happy and harmonious life is to understand that what was, what is, and what will be all follow universal laws. One such law worth understanding is that you must accept things just as they are, rather than wishing them to be different.

Humans, other living creatures, and even the four elements are transformed and changed upward and downward, as earth becomes water, water transforms into air, and air turns to ether. In the same way, transformation takes place from above in a downward direction. If you turn and focus your mind toward these things and persuade yourself to accept your own free will, you'll live a great life.

Fragment 8

When you hear a thundering sound from the sky that surprises you, or you receive news of a tornado touching down in your town, even if you're the most conscious person you're bound to be affected, and you may shrink back and grow pale for a moment. This isn't because you've made a rational judgment that something bad is about to happen, but because the logical part of your brain is confused and short-circuited, and you've gone into a primitive survival mode.

Very soon, however, you regain control of your thoughts and you have the ability to reject your fears completely. Many say that this is the main difference between the mind of the foolish and the conscious person. The foolish one thinks that his first impressions really are what they appear to be. But the conscious individual, although initially affected, keeps consistency and firmness of judgment. He need not fear these impressions and realizes that to do so is to maintain a false face and harbor empty terror.

FRAGMENT 9

Most people who seem to be practicing philosophy are "all words, no action." Once there was a man who talked a good talk but had lost all sense of healthy shame. He had misguided energy, bad habits, and exaggerated self-confidence. He relied on his power of speech. This man concentrated on everything except his moral character. On the surface, he was doing all the right things, such as tackling philosophical subjects, even physics. I said to him, "Hey, how are you integrating all this knowledge you claim to possess? Look inside yourself. Are you putting it into an unclean vessel? If you are, then this wisdom will be ruined. It'll become urine or vinegar, or perhaps something even worse."

This is a key teaching of mine, namely that when philosophy or conscious-living principles are poured into a dirty and corrupt container, the contents are altered, changed, and spoiled.

There are really only two vices that are more important and offensive than all others: first, your inability to put up with things; and second, your inability to control yourself. Let's convert these two vices into ideals. You must accept things as they are and let go of those beyond your control. You should also understand your desires and pleasures and maintain mastery of them, rather than let them run over you. If you can do so, then you'll certainly be largely faultless and live a most peaceful life.

FRAGMENT 10

Archelaus once sent a messenger to summon Socrates. He promised to make the philosopher rich. Upon hearing this, Socrates told the messenger to take back this reply: "Four quarts of barley meal can be bought at Athens for an obol [an ancient Greek coin of little value], and the springs run with water. What I now possess is sufficient for me. Do you remember that Polus acted the same way toward Oedipus when he was king as he did when Oedipus was a vagrant and beggar? Be like Polus! Or, better yet, imitate Odysseus, who wasn't any less distinguished in rags than he was in fine purple robes."

Fragment 11

Beware of passive-aggressive people. Although they don't seem angry on the surface, they act in the same way as those who are completely carried away by their rage. You should guard yourself against them, because when people express their displeasure overtly, the feelings move through them quickly. But when emotions are bottled up, they last a long time.

FRAGMENT 12

Once I was asked, "There are many people who live in integrity and are noble and good who also die of hunger and cold. How do you explain this?"

I replied: "Those who blame God because the wicked aren't suffering as they should be are acting as if they were punished because their fingernails are clean, which is absurd. I say there's a big difference between virtue and property."

FRAGMENT 13

Some philosophers think that pleasure isn't natural, but rather something that results from justice, self-control, and freedom. Nature has given you a gauge to tell you when you're out of integrity with respect to your experience and expression of pleasure: It's your healthy sense of shame. I often blush when I catch myself saying something shameful. It's this emotion that won't allow me to accept all pleasure as good.

FRAGMENT 14

Worthwhile philosophy stresses that you shouldn't even stretch out a finger without good reason.

FRAGMENT 15

It's not easy to live consciously unless you hear and speak the principles every day, and at the same time, apply them in your life.

FRAGMENT 16

When you go to a play, you usually accept the performance that you get. If you were to ask the actors to also give you some fish and a cake, everyone would think your request was absurd. Yet in real life, you often ask God for what hasn't been given to you, and continue to do so in spite of the evidence of how much you already have.

Fragment 17

"I'm better than you," declares one person, "because I own lots of real estate and you can't even afford to eat."

"Well I'm terrific-looking, so I'm superior to you," replies another.

Yet one horse doesn't boast to the next, "I'm greater than you because I have a shinier coat, plenty of fodder, and gold bridles and embroidered saddles." And the other doesn't say in return, "But I'm a lot faster."

Every creature's worth is measured by its own morality or vice. Are humans the only creatures that have no virtue? How absurd to instead value hair, rank, and accomplishments!

FRAGMENT 18

People who are sick don't want physicians who offer no advice. They think they're disinterested or have given up on them. Then why shouldn't you assume the same attitude toward a philosopher or teacher and conclude he isn't supporting your right way of thinking when he doesn't tell you anything of real value?

People in good physical health are able to withstand greater stress, heat, and cold than those with poor or mediocre health. Likewise, people whose souls are in good shape can bear anger, grief, excessive joy, and all other emotions.

FRAGMENT 19

Agrippinus was a great man of character and integrity. Although he had lots of money, he never bragged. In fact, he even blushed when another praised him. He was a man of such virtue that he could write an essay of appreciation about every hardship that ever happened to him. For example, if he had a fever, he would appreciate that he wasn't cold. If someone criticized him, he would appreciate the opportunity to improve himself. If he were banished, he appreciated discovering new lands. Once, when he was about to sit down for dinner, a messenger interrupted with news that Nero had ordered him to go into exile. "Well, then," he said, "we will dine in Aricia."

As governor, Agrippinus would try to persuade people whom he was sentencing that it was in their best interest to be punished. "For it isn't as your enemy," he said, "that I hand down this proclamation, but as your protector and guardian—as a surgeon who encourages a man who has asked him to operate to try alternative forms of treatment first."

FRAGMENT 20

Nature is admirable, and as Xenophon said, "fond of her creatures." Most of us love our bodies and take care of them, even though of all things, they're the most filthy and require the most upkeep. If you don't believe me, try just for five days to take care of your neighbor's body. I don't think you could do it. Imagine what it would be like to get up in the morning, clean his teeth, take him to the bathroom, and bathe and wash him. In reality, it's indeed wonderful that you love something that demands such care and attention day after day. You stuff the sack, then you empty it again. What a pain! But you must serve God; therefore, you must bear washing, feeding, and sheltering this paltry and miserable body.

When you die, and nature, which gave you your form, takes it away, will you try to argue? "I love my body," you protest. It isn't nature that gives you that love, yet it's nature that says, "Let it go now, and suffer no more."

FRAGMENT 21

People are extraordinary: They wish to neither live nor die. If a man dies young, we blame God, saying, "He passed away before his time." If a woman fails to die when she's old, she, too, blames God. At the time when she should be resting, she's encumbered with the troubles of living. Then, when death approaches, she wishes to live again, and enlists doctors and hospitals and spares no cost trying to keep herself alive.

FRAGMENT 22

When you have to confront someone or be aggressive, remember to tell yourself beforehand that you aren't a wild animal. Then you'll never do anything savagely, and you'll live your entire life without having to repent or account for your actions afterward.

FRAGMENT 23

Are you a little spirit hauling around a big corpse, or are you a big spirit hauling around a little corpse?

FRAGMENT 24

Just as a large ship shouldn't have a tiny anchor, a life shouldn't cling to one single hope. Both for your legs and dreams, possibility should govern your stride.

FRAGMENT 25

It's better for the soul to be healed than the body, because it's better to die than live badly.

Fragment 26

The pleasures that come least often are those that delight us most.

FRAGMENT 27

Truth is eternal. Unlike beauty, it doesn't fade; and unlike freedom of speech, it can't be taken away by any government. Truth gives you all that is just, lawful, and right.

PART III

HOW TO PUT EPICTETUS'S PRINCIPLES TO WORK FOR YOU

THE MASTER-KEY
EXPERIENTIAL ACTIVITY

Your understanding and appreciation of Epictetus's message will likely take a quantum leap if you take the time to go through the following activity carefully and thoughtfully. We call it the Master-Key Experiential Activity because like a master key, it fits many different doors, and you can carry it easily in your pocket anywhere you go. Also like a master key, it can open many treasure-filled rooms in the magnificent mansion of life.

Set aside 30 minutes to an hour to do this activity. Based on our experience in teaching it to thousands of people, as well as using it ourselves for many years, we can promise you that the time and energy you devote to it will be richly rewarded.

Getting Started

When you're feeling stuck, it's usually because you're focusing on something that you can't control. When you shift your attention to something you can actually change, you'll usually feel an immediate increase in your peace of mind. You'll often see an instantaneous improvement in the situation as well. Letting go of things you have no authority over is the primary tool for freeing yourself from inner agitation, just as working on things within your power is your primary tool for making a positive difference in your world.

To help you make this important shift, we've devised a simple exercise. Begin by imagining two separate files. You might picture two manila folders, for example, or two steel file cabinets. Some people prefer to think of two folders on the desktop of their computer. If you're a touch-oriented person, you can even use a couple of real file folders that you can hold in your hands. The type you visualize is up to you—all that's important is that you clearly establish two distinct files in your awareness.

Next, clearly identify one file as "Things I Absolutely Can Change" and the second as "Things I Absolutely Can't Change." As you now know, that unpleasant feeling of drained exhaustion that many people feel is the direct result of putting too much attention on the "Can't Change" file. Here are some items that belong there (do any of these apply to you?):

- What other people think about you

- Unpleasant things that happened in the past

- The feelings of other people

- The future

As you can see, all these items clearly belong in your "Can't Change" file. For example, none of us have any say over what other people think about us. What you do have control over, though, is whether you pick up the phone and ask someone, "How do you feel about me?"

From 35 years of practical experience as therapists and helping professionals, we can tell you for certain that many people spend thousands of hours worrying about what someone else believes about them, without ever taking the simple step of asking!

Now let's contrast items in your "Can't Change" file with some similar ones that could go in your "Can Change" file. Here are several things that are completely within your power to control:

- Communicating your authentic feelings and thoughts to your partner

- Taking a specific action to make amends for past wrongs

- Doing something today that might contribute to a positive future

All these items are well within your ability to manage. The amount of energy required to take these steps is the same amount (if not less) that many people squander in fretting about things they have no authority over.

The Next Step

Now let's extend what you've learned so far into other crucial areas of your life. For this step you'll need a few blank sheets of paper and something to write with. Even if you're a die-hard computer user, we recommend doing this part by hand so that you have the physical feel of locating each item in its proper file.

On your first sheet of paper, make an outline that looks like the one on the next page:

Sorting My Two Files

File One: Can Change	Items to Sort	File Two: Can't Change
	My feelings	
	Other people's feelings	
	What I did in the past	
	What other people do	
	What other people accomplish	
	What I accomplish	
	My waist size today	
	What I swallow today	
	What I do for exercise today	
	What I say to people	

Now, physically cross off each one as you relocate it into the correct file. For example, put a line through "My feelings" and rewrite it in your "Can't Change" file. Are you surprised that it belongs there? We were, too, when we first realized it, but it's absolutely true. Think about it: If you're scared, you can't change it because it's already there. You might be able to train yourself not to be afraid in the future, but right now, you are.

It's best not to put energy into controlling your emotions, but rather to put it into being honest with yourself and others. You don't choose most of your feelings of dislike or like either. If you don't like oysters, for example, you can't really help it. You might be able to train yourself to like them, but it would be because you did things in your "Can Change" file, such as eating five oysters every day for a week.

Likewise, it may come as a shock to you that none of us has any control over our weight. If you don't believe this fact, stand on a set of scales and try to lose five pounds. Watch the numbers carefully. The needle doesn't move. Although this may sound silly, it points to a real problem: Many people put so much worry into how much they weigh and what size they are that they don't have the energy to exercise and put the right foods in their mouths every day.

For starters, then, be sure to put "My waist size today" in your "Can't Change" file. Put "What I swallow today" in your "Can Change" file.

Now consider the "Items to Sort," and physically relocate each one into the correct file. When you're finished, you'll have a sheet that looks something like this:

Sorting My Two Files

File One: Can Change	File Two: Can't Change
What I swallow today	My feelings
What I do for exercise today	Other people's feelings
What I say to people	What I did in the past
What I accomplish	What other people do
	What other people accomplish
	My waist size today

Which ones seemed obvious to you and which ones seemed ambiguous? Take some time to reflect on this. Select one of the items that was confusing and delve into it more deeply, asking yourself detailed questions about it. For example, if you found it surprising that "What I did in the past" is outside your control, you might ask yourself what it is about your history that you feel the need to change. Here are some sample questions that have proved illuminating to some people:

- What specifically about this issue do I most want to control?

- What about this issue do I wish had been different?

- How am I holding my well-being and happiness hostage to this issue? (For example, have you stopped improving yourself spiritually because you're too worried about what other people will think?)

Make several additional sheets with your two files listed on them. Post them in various places such as on your refrigerator, in your car, and on your bathroom mirror. Over the coming days and weeks, add as many things as you can think of to your list, sorting each of them into the correct file.

Going Forward

You'll likely find it valuable to extend this activity into the world of your close relationships. Many people make themselves miserable by trying to control or change the feelings and behavior of other people. It comes as a great relief when you fully realize that while you can certainly influence others, you have no ability to change them. They have to do that for themselves.

In conflicted relationships, there's usually one person who takes too much responsibility for things and one person who takes too little. Relationships only work well when both people agree to be 100 percent accountable. The first step in attaining that equal state is for both people to let go of trying to control the other.

As you work on these concepts, be sure to give yourself plenty of loving acceptance. It never does any good to criticize or shame yourself for the things you discover as you do this or any other transformational process. Just take it one step at a time, one day at a time, one moment at a time. Eventually, by applying this activity in a disciplined yet gentle manner, you can make remarkable strides in productivity and peace of mind.

ABOUT THE AUTHORS

Gay Hendricks is the author of more than 25 books dealing with personal and relationship transformation, including *Conscious Loving* (co-authored with his wife, Dr. Kathlyn Hendricks), *Learning to Love Yourself,* and *Conscious Living.* He received his Ph.D. in counseling psychology from Stanford University and taught for 21 years at the University of Colorado before founding The Hendricks Institute (**www.hendricks.com**). He and Kathlyn make their home in Ojai, California. They are also co-founders, along with Stephen Simon, of The Spiritual Cinema Circle.

Philip Johncock is an author, coach, and consultant who lives near Reno, Nevada. He's the author of *Dream-Making to Billions,* a book on the art of grant writing. Website: **www.johncock.com**

We hope you enjoyed this Hay House book. If you'd like to receive
a free catalog featuring additional Hay House books and products, or if
you'd like information about the Hay Foundation, please contact:

Hay House, Inc.
P.O. Box 5100
Carlsbad, CA 92018-5100

(760) 431-7695 or **(800) 654-5126**
(760) 431-6948 (fax) or **(800) 650-5115 (fax)**
www.hayhouse.com® • **www.hayfoundation.org**

Published and distributed in Australia by: Hay House Australia Pty. Ltd. •
18/36 Ralph St. • Alexandria NSW 2015 • *Phone:* 612-9669-4299 •
Fax: 612-9669-4144 • www.hayhouse.com.au

Published and distributed in the United Kingdom by: Hay House UK, Ltd. •
Unit 62, Canalot Studios • 292 Kensal Rd., London W10 5BE • *Phone:* 44-20-8962-1230
• *Fax:* 44-20-8962-1239 • www.hayhouse.co.uk

Published and distributed in the Republic of South Africa by:
Hay House SA (Pty), Ltd., P.O. Box 990, Witkoppen 2068 •
Phone/Fax: 27-11-706-6612 • orders@psdprom.co.za

Published in India by: Hay House Publications (India) Pvt. Ltd.
www.hayhouseindia.co.in

Distributed in India by: Media Star, 7 Vaswani Mansion, 120 Dinshaw
Vachha Rd., Churchgate, Mumbai 400020 • *Phone:* 91 (22) 22815538-39-40 •
Fax: 91 (22) 22839619 • booksdivision@mediastar.co.in

Distributed in Canada by: Raincoast • 9050 Shaughnessy St., Vancouver, B.C.
V6P 6E5 • *Phone:* (604) 323-7100 • *Fax:* (604) 323-2600 • www.raincoast.com

Tune in to **HayHouseRadio.com**® for the best in inspirational talk radio featuring top Hay House authors! And, sign up via the Hay House USA Website to receive the Hay House online newsletter and stay informed about what's going on with your favorite authors. You'll receive bimonthly announcements about: Discounts and Offers, Special Events, Product Highlights, Free Excerpts, Giveaways, and more!

www.hayhouse.com®